The Dinosaur Museum

by JoAnn Early Macken

amicus readers

1

Amicus Readers are published by Amicus
P.O. Box 1329 Mankato, Minnesota 56002

Printed in the United States of America
at Corporate Graphics, North Mankato,
Minnesota.

Library of Congress Cataloging-in-
Publication Data
Macken, JoAnn Early, 1953-
  The dinosaur museum / by JoAnn Early Macken.
    p. cm. -- (Amicus readers. My community)
  Summary: "Describes how dinosaur fossils are
found, prepared, and displayed in museums,
and what you might see at a dinosaur museum.
Includes visual literacy activity"-- Provided by publisher.
  Includes index.
  ISBN 978-1-60753-023-7 (lib. bdg.)
  1. Paleontology--Museums--Juvenile literature. 2. Natural history
museums--Collection management--Juvenile literature. I. Title.
  QE716.A1M33 2011
  567.9074--dc22

                        2010010554

Series Editor   Rebecca Glaser
Series Designer   Mary Herrmann
Book Designer   Mary Herrmann
Photo Researcher   Heather Dreisbach

Photo Credits
Alamy/David Davis Photoproductions, 13, 21 (t); Alamy/Gary
Crabbe, 15, 20 (t), 21 (b); Corbis/Tranz, 7, 9, 11, 20 (m, b), 21 (m);
Getty/Stephen Wilkes, 19; iStock/Brandon Smith, 5; iStockphoto/
breckeni, cover, 1; Krechet/Dreamstime.com, multiple pages
(watermark); Photo Researchers/Roger Harris, 17

1223
42010
10 9 8 7 6 5 4 3 2 1

Contents

At a dinosaur museum, you can see dinosaur fossils. Fossils are thousands of years old. They are found under the ground.

fossil

Scientists dig for dinosaur bones and teeth. These are fossils. A scientist clears off the dirt with a knife.

bone →

A scientist cleans the fossils. He chips off dirt with a hammer and chisel.

chisel →

9

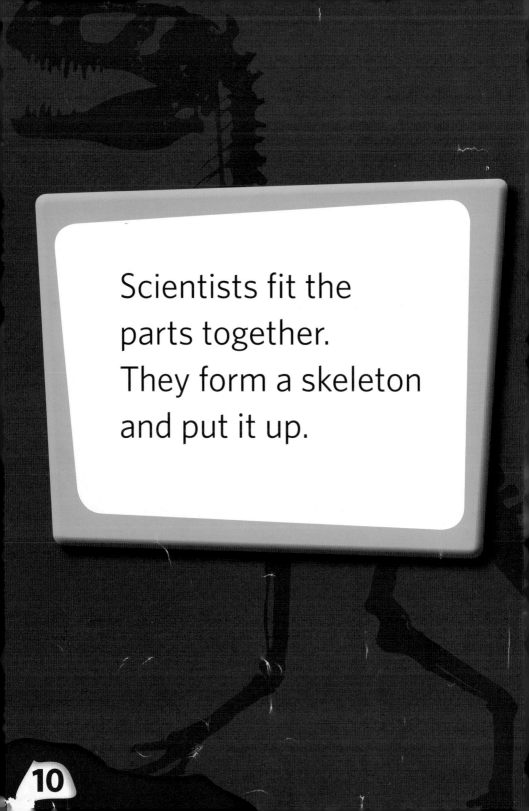

Scientists fit the parts together. They form a skeleton and put it up.

skeleton

11

Scientists make dinosaur models based on the shape of skeletons. But what color was a dinosaur's skin? No one knows.

model

At a dinosaur museum, you can learn about types of dinosaurs. *Tyrannosaurus Rex* was huge. Its teeth are the size of bananas!

teeth

Not all dinosaurs were big. *Compsognathus* was only as big as a turkey. It ate small lizards.

In a dinosaur museum, you can touch real fossils. You can learn how dinosaurs lived and died.

Picture Glossary

 **bone**—a part of an animal's skeleton

 **chisel**—a tool with a flat, sharp end used to chip away dirt and stone from fossils

 **fossil**—a part or trace of plant or animal life from long ago, such as a footprint, a shell, or a bone

model—something that is built to show an example of how it looks

skeleton—the bony structure of an animal

teeth—the hard structures an animal uses to bite and chew

Dinosaur Puzzler: A Second Look

Take a second look at the photos in the book to answer these questions.

1. How is a model different from a fossil?

2. What things are the same between *Tyrannosaurus Rex* and *Compsognathus*?

3. How do museum workers clean a large skeleton?

Check your answers on page 24.

Ideas for Parents and Teachers

My Community, an Amicus Readers Level 1 series, provides essential support for new readers while exploring children's first frame of reference, the community. Photo labels and a picture glossary help readers connect words and images. The activity page teaches visual literacy and critical thinking skills. Use the following strategies to engage your children or students.

Before Reading

- Ask children to tell you what they know about dinosaurs and museums. Ask them if they've been to a museum before.
- Look at the photos. Ask children to describe what they see.
- Look at the picture glossary together. Read and discuss the words.

While Reading

- Ask the children to read the book independently. Provide support as needed.
- Help them use the photo labels and picture glossary to understand unfamiliar words.

After Reading

- Ask children how scientists find fossils and how museum workers prepare exhibits.
- Have children answer the questions in the activity on page 22.
- Ask the children to think further with questions such as: *Did all dinosaurs eat meat? How do scientists know about dinosaurs?*

INDEX

WEB SITES

The Dino Reserve
http://www.kbears.com/dinosaurs/index.html

Dinosaur Floor: Meet the Dinosaurs
http://www.cotf.edu/ete/modules/msese/dinosaurflr/
diorama.html

New Mexico Museum of Natural History and Science
http://www.nmnaturalhistory.org/trex/images.html

ANSWERS FROM PAGE 22

1. Models have skin and are built by scientists.
   Fossils are bone and found underground.
2. Both walk on two legs and have short arms.
3. They use a vacuum cleaner.